Soul Retreats™

_____

Presented To

_____

Presented By

_____

Date

Soul Retreats™ for Busy People
ISBN 0-310-98900-0

Copyright 2002 by GRQ Ink, Inc.
1948 Green Hills Boulevard
Franklin, Tennessee 37067

"Soul Retreats" is a trademark owned by GRQ, Inc.

Published by Inspirio™, The gift group of Zondervan
5300 Patterson Avenue, SE
Grand Rapids, Michigan 49530

Requests for information should be addressed to:
Inspirio™, The gift group of Zondervan
Grand Rapids, Michigan 49530

http://www.inspiriogifts.com

Editor and Compiler: Lila Empson
Associate Editor: Janice Jacobson
Project Manager: Tom Dean
Manuscript written and prepared by Rebecca Currington in conjunction with
Snapdragon Editorial Group, Inc.
Design: Whisner Design Group

Soul Retreats™
for Busy People

inspirio™

Contents

Introduction

You are capable and responsible; perhaps that's why you are so busy. But do you find it too easy to become swept up in the demands of the day and press forward despite sometimes overwhelming conditions? Like your body, your soul needs care.

Give yourself a break, a needed retreat. Because of your busy life, this may seem impossible at times. But taking care of one's soul doesn't have to mean making room for a vacation at the beach or a mountain resort. The resilient human soul can make retreat in brief moments of solitude and contemplation.

Make time today to give your soul a retreat. Begin at the first retreat and meditate your way through the retreats in order. Or choose from among the thirty fifteen-minute retreats and select one that suits your needs for today.

Rest Where You Are

When, spurred by tasks unceasing or undone, you would seek rest afar,
And cannot, though repose be rightly won—Rest where you are.

Neglect the needless; sanctify the rest; move without stress or jar;
With quiet of a spirit self-possessed—Rest where you are.

Not in event, restriction, or release, not in scenes near or far,
But in ourselves are restlessness or peace—Rest where you are.

Where lives the soul lives God; His day, His world, no phantom mists need mar;
His starry nights are tents of peace unfurled—Rest where you are.

Author Unknown

The Power of Prayer

A Moment to Pause Meditative prayer offers a great respite for the soul. It soothes and comforts us as we lay down our concerns and rest quietly in the presence of our great and mighty God.

Morning, noon, or night—the time of day you choose to pray doesn't matter. The place where you pray doesn't matter much either, as long as it's quiet, peaceful, and as private as possible. Just close your eyes and focus your attention completely on God. Actively consider the majesty of the earth he has created. As the images of snowcapped mountains, ocean breakers, brilliant sunsets, delicate seashells, and brightly blossoming flowers come to mind, thank God for each image.

As you consider the wonders of God's greatness, release yourself into his care. Consciously remind yourself that the God who keeps the sun, moon, and stars moving in their orbits, the God who created the earth and all its wonders, is more than able to guard and keep you.

Come away from your prayerful minutes at your desk, on your porch, or in your favorite chair strengthened and rested.

Prayer is ordained to this end that we should confess our needs to God, and bare our hearts to him, as children lay their troubles in full confidence before their parents.
—John Calvin

A Moment to Reflect

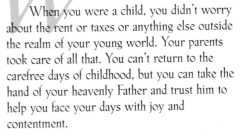

When you were a child, you didn't worry about the rent or taxes or anything else outside the realm of your young world. Your parents took care of all that. You can't return to the carefree days of childhood, but you can take the hand of your heavenly Father and trust him to help you face your days with joy and contentment.

If you are feeling overwhelmed by the demands of your hectic life, God wants you to know that he is ready to come alongside and help you sort through the clutter. Together you can achieve a balanced lifestyle that includes rest and relaxation.

There is an hour of calm relief
From every throbbing care;
'Tis when before a throne of grace,
I kneel in secret prayer,
When one by one, like threads of gold,
The hues of twilight fall,
Oh, sweet communion with my God,
My Saviour and my all!

—*FANNY J. CROSBY*

9

*Let us...approach the throne of grace with
boldness, so that we may receive mercy and
find grace to help in time of need.*

Hebrews 4:16 NRSV

A Moment to Refresh

*Very early in the morning, while it was still
dark, Jesus got up, left the house and went off to
a solitary place, where he prayed.*

Mark 1:35

*Don't worry about anything, but in all your
prayers ask God for what you need, always
asking him with a thankful heart.*

Philippians 4:6 GNT

*Evening, morning and noon
I cry out in distress,
and God hears my voice.*

Psalm 55:17

*I lift up my eyes to the hills—
where does my help come from?
My help comes from the LORD,
the Maker of heaven and earth.*

Psalm 121:1–2

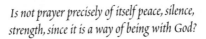

*Is not prayer precisely of itself peace, silence,
strength, since it is a way of being with God?*

&

—JACQUES ILLUL

*I cry aloud to the LORD;
I lift up my voice to the LORD for mercy.
I pour out my complaint before him;
before him I tell my trouble.
When my spirit grows faint within me,
it is you who know my way.*

Psalm 142:1–3

*The effectual fervent prayer of a righteous
man availeth much.*

James 5:16 KJV

*When you pray, go into your room, close
the door and pray to your Father, who is
unseen. Then your Father, who sees what is
done in secret, will reward you.*

Matthew 6:6

*Pray in the Spirit on all occasions with all
kinds of prayers and requests.*

Ephesians 6:18

*Prayer serves as an
edge and border to
preserve the web of
life from unraveling.*

&

—ROBERT HALL

Soaking It Up!

A Moment to Pause

Though they typically take a bit longer than a shower, baths are a wonderful way to relax. Turn off the phone and lock the door so you won't be disturbed, and retreat from the world for a few minutes. Then climb in and slip down into the warm, soothing water. Allow the water to cover you all the way to your chin like a warm comforter.

Close your eyes and let your mind drift away from problems, cares, and concerns. As you feel your body relaxing, focus your mind on God. Ask him to cleanse you from every unhealthy thought or action and refresh and restore your soul with thoughts of goodness, gentleness, joy, and peace.

A brisk shower cleanses and comforts the body, but taking time for a warm bath provides an opportunity to cleanse and comfort the soul.

Lingering in a warm bath may not be possible every day. But try to sneak away a couple of times a week or on the weekend. Enjoy the feeling of being clean and refreshed inside as well as out.

Bathe twice a day to be really clean,
once a day to be passably clean,
once a week to avoid being a public menace.
——Anthony Burgess

A Moment to Reflect

Our culture has moved from slow-moving buggy to supersonic jet, from snail-mail to e-mail, from home-cooked meals eaten around the table to fast food eaten on the run. And all this change has taken place in little more than a generation.

Should we revert to the slower lifestyles we used to embrace? No, but some activities are worth reviving. Years ago, people did what they had to do. We, on the other hand, are able to do what we want. Make some time to slow down and soak it up!

Released

If only for these rare and fleeting moments
I remove from myself all that clings to me,
Harries my thoughts, and burdens my soul when I
Fall into the water's warm embrace; released
Like a child from her mother's womb,
I emerge from my private baptism
And life greets me anew.

—*Tara Afriat*

13

Cleanse me with hyssop,
and I will be clean, O Lord;
wash me, and I will be whiter than snow.

Psalm 51:7

A Moment to Refresh

As water reflects the face,
so a man's heart reflects the man.

Proverbs 27:19

Let us purify ourselves from everything that
makes body or soul unclean, and let us be
completely holy by living in awe of God.

2 Corinthians 7:1 GNT

Let us draw near to God with a sincere heart in
full assurance of faith, having our hearts
sprinkled to cleanse us from a guilty conscience
and having our bodies washed with pure water.

Hebrews 10:22

Christ loved the church and gave himself up for
her to make her holy, cleansing her by the
washing with water through the word.

Ephesians 5:25–26

Christ is the God over all, who has arranged to wash away sin from mankind, rendering the old man new.

—HIPPOLYTUS

The LORD has dealt with me according to
my righteousness;
according to the cleanness of my hands he
has rewarded me.

Psalm 18:20

Have mercy upon me, O God, according to
thy lovingkindness: according unto the
multitude of thy tender mercies blot out my
transgressions. Wash me thoroughly from
mine iniquity, and cleanse me from my sin.

Psalm 51:1–2 KJV

If we confess our sins, he is faithful and just
to forgive us our sins, and to cleanse us
from all unrighteousness.

1 John 1:9 KJV

Water clear,
standing near,
Wash our hands
and faces clean.
May the Lord, by
His Word,
Wash our hearts
from every sin.
So let everything
we see
Turn our thoughts,
O Lord, to Thee.

—PHILIP P. BLISS

Words That Inspire

A Moment to Pause

Nothing melts away stress like a good book. Whether you wish to be inspired, instructed, or just plain entertained, a book can lift you up and away from the cares of your busy day and escort you into a world of beauty and adventure.

But where does a busy person like you find the time to slip away into the magic of a book? You shouldn't worry about being able to finish a whole book or even a chapter in one sitting. If you have fifteen minutes, then fifteen minutes is all you need. Pick up your book and read as much as time allows. It's okay if it takes weeks or even months to finish a book.

The type of reading you choose is completely up to you as well. You may prefer the blatant escapism provided by a good novel. You may enjoy the orderly inspiration of a beautiful gift book. Perhaps you are drawn to the enrichment offered by nonfiction. Whatever your tastes, choose something that captures your interest and inspires you.

The great thing about reading is that you can do it almost anywhere: in the car while you're waiting to pick up your children, in the doctor's office as you patiently wait to be seen, at your desk during a work break. Wherever you choose, a refreshing retreat for your soul awaits.

Read to refill the wells of inspiration.
—Harold J. Ockenga

A Moment to Reflect

Reading provides a joyous retreat from the frantic busyness of your day. It can take you to exotic faraway places and can fill you with a sense of wonder. It can encourage your faith in God and lift your perspective. Reading can rest and relax your soul.

When you feel the busyness of your day closing in on you, when you need a spurt of inspiration or a nudge of creativity, stop for a few minutes and give your heart, mind, and body a mini-vacation in the wonderful world of words.

The Manuscripts of God

And nature, the old nurse, took
The child upon her knee,
Saying, "Here is a story book
My father hath writ for thee.
Come wander with me," she said,
"In regions yet untrod
And read what is still unread
In the manuscripts of God."

—Henry Wadsworth Longfellow

My eyes stay open
through the watches of the night,
that I may meditate on your promises, O LORD.

Psalm 119:148

A Moment to Refresh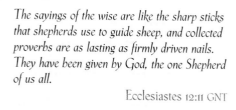

The sayings of the wise are like the sharp sticks
that shepherds use to guide sheep, and collected
proverbs are as lasting as firmly driven nails.
They have been given by God, the one Shepherd
of us all.

Ecclesiastes 12:11 GNT

Happy is the one who reads this book, and
happy are those who listen to the words of this
prophetic message and obey what is written in
this book! For the time is near when all these
things will happen.

Revelation 1:3 GNT

Pleasant words are a honeycomb,
sweet to the soul and healing to the bones.

Proverbs 16:24

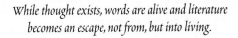

While thought exists, words are alive and literature becomes an escape, not from, but into living.

—CYRIL CONNOLLY

All Scripture is God-breathed and is useful for teaching, rebuking, correcting and training in righteousness, so that the man of God may be thoroughly equipped for every good work.

2 Timothy 3:16–17

The wise in heart are called discerning, and pleasant words promote instruction.

Proverbs 16:21

Everything that was written in the past was written to teach us, so that through endurance and the encouragement of the Scriptures we might have hope.

Romans 15:4

A book is like a garden carried in the pocket.

—ANCIENT PROVERB

Walk It Off

A Moment to Pause   Walking—we park close in to avoid it. Yet there are few better ways to calm your emotions and rest your mind than a good, brisk walk. Take it slow at first, and head out, with no particular destination in mind. Walk for the simple joy of it.

As you walk along, focus on the sensation of your blood coursing through your veins—proof positive that you're alive. Lift your head and thank God for your life. Notice your muscles as they flex in your arms and legs. Lift your head and thank God for your strength. Feel the warmth in your face—a sign that your body is responding as it should. Lift your head and thank God for your health.

Adam walked with God in the cool of the evening, but the time of day isn't what made that activity so special. It was the interaction enjoyed by Creator and created. As you walk, take advantage of the time to fellowship with your Creator. Tell him you're glad to be alive.

Walk until you feel invigorated in your body and your soul.

Two legs with which to walk about on God's green earth—
what greater store of blessing could be imagined.
—Roberta S. Cully

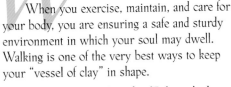

A Moment to Reflect

When you exercise, maintain, and care for your body, you are ensuring a safe and sturdy environment in which your soul may dwell. Walking is one of the very best ways to keep your "vessel of clay" in shape.

Walking is most beneficial when it's done on a regular basis. Start out with twenty or thirty minutes three times a week. Many busy people find that they are more successful if they walk first thing in the morning, before beginning their workday. If it's a new activity for you, resist the urge to walk too far too fast. Over time, your body will adjust to the exertion. Your strength and stamina will increase, your muscles will lose the ache and begin to hum, and your soul will shout for the joy of walking with God.

Walk quietly—
And know that He is God.
When evening shadows lie against the hill—
In the hush of twilight, when the world is still.
And the balm of peace soothes every ill—
Walk quietly.

—AUTHOR UNKNOWN

*You have delivered me from death
and my feet from stumbling,
that I may walk before God
in the light of life.*

Psalm 56:13

A Moment to Refresh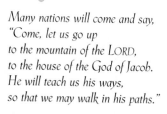

*Many nations will come and say,
"Come, let us go up
to the mountain of the LORD,
to the house of the God of Jacob.
He will teach us his ways,
so that we may walk in his paths."*

Micah 4:2

*You show me the path of life, O LORD.
In your presence there is fullness of joy;
in your right hand are pleasures forevermore.*

Psalm 16:11 NRSV

*Jesus said, "I am the light of the world.
Whoever follows me will never walk in
darkness, but will have the light of life."*

John 8:12

Take God for your bridegroom and friend, and walk with him continually; and you will not sin and will learn to love, and the things you must do will work out prosperously for you.

—JOHN OF THE CROSS

Whoever claims to live in him must walk as Jesus did.

1 John 2:6

Teach me your way, O LORD; lead me in a straight path.

Psalm 27:11

I guide you in the way of wisdom and lead you along straight paths. When you walk, your steps will not be hampered; when you run, you will not stumble.

Proverbs 4:11–12

The Lord said, "I will look upon you with favor and make you fruitful and increase your numbers, and I will keep my covenant with you.... I will walk among you and be your God, and you will be my people."

Leviticus 26:9, 12

We do not walk to God with the feet of our body, nor would wings, if we had them, carry us to Him, but we go to Him, by the affections of our soul.

—AUGUSTINE OF HIPPO

Like a Playful Child

A Moment to Pause

Children are masters of play. They take life as they find it and allow their imaginations to fill in the blanks. What other explanation can there be for their ability to sit happily in the dirt for hours with nothing more than a stick? How else could they transform a box into a cave or a car or a cruise ship? How else could they take a blanket and "see" a tent, a superhero cape, a landscape for a village?

Take a break from your busy schedule and make your way to a place where children are at play. Get down on the floor, go out into the yard, hop on the merry-go-round at the park, throw a few snowballs or spitballs. Or perch on a park bench and imagine yourself entering in and playing among them.

Let your body and mind relax as you enter the carefree world of childhood. For a few short minutes, shake off the responsibilities and refinements of adulthood and allow your heart to run barefoot, free, and happy in the tall, green grass. Reflect with delight on the fact that you are indeed a child—a child of God.

One laugh of a child will make the holiest day
more sacred.
—Robert Green Ingersoll

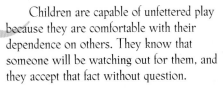

A Moment to Reflect

Children are capable of unfettered play because they are comfortable with their dependence on others. They know that someone will be watching out for them, and they accept that fact without question.

If the responsibilities of your grown–up world keep you running in circles, spinning plates, and trying to hold all the aspects of your life together, visualize yourself as a child at play under the watchful eye of your heavenly Father. Forget your tension. Let worries drain away. Deliberately relax your shoulders, relax your stance, let your limbs hang loose. Know that God, who is more dependable than any earthly parent could ever be, is always looking out for you. So play! Enjoy God's world.

Our religion is one which challenges the ordinary human standards by holding that the ideal of life is the spirit of a little child. We tend to glorify adulthood and wisdom and worldly prudence, but the gospel reverses all this. The gospel says that the inescapable condition of entrance into the divine fellowship is that we turn and become as a little child.

—*Elton Trueblood*

As a father has compassion on his children,
so the LORD has compassion on those
who fear him.

Psalm 103:13

A Moment to Refresh

Some people brought children to Jesus for him
to place his hands on them, but the disciples
scolded the people. When Jesus noticed this, he
was angry and said to his disciples, "Let the
children come to me, and do not stop them,
because the Kingdom of God belongs to such as
these."

Mark 10:13-14 GNT

Jesus called a little child and had him stand
among them. And he said: "I tell you the truth,
unless you change and become like little
children, you will never enter the kingdom of
heaven."

Matthew 18:2-3

How excellent is thy loving-kindness, O God!
therefore the children of men put their trust
under the shadow of thy wings.

Psalm 36:7 KJV

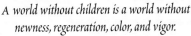

A world without children is a world without newness, regeneration, color, and vigor.

—James C. Dobson

Come, my children, listen to me;
I will teach you the fear of the LORD.
Psalm 34:11

My heart is not proud, O LORD,
my eyes are not haughty;
I do not concern myself with great matters
or things too wonderful for me.
But I have stilled and quieted my soul;
like a weaned child with its mother,
like a weaned child is my soul within me.
Psalm 131:1–2

The soul is healed by being with children.

—Fyodor Dostoevsky

How great is the love the Father has
lavished on us, that we should be called
children of God! And that is what we are!
1 John 3:1

Jesus took the children in his arms, put his
hands on them and blessed them.
Mark 10:16

Wonder and Awe

A Moment to Pause

Viewing the heavens that God has created is an inspiring exercise. Slip away one warm, clear night and throw a blanket on the ground. Lie there in the darkness, take in the broad expanse of the sky, and watch as dancing dots of brilliant light shimmer above, beneath, and around the silver orb of the moon. In comparison to such a startling display, problems often appear small and inconsequential, and possibilities great and unlimited.

On colder nights, wrap yourself in a blanket and sit on a lawn chair with a cup of coffee or hot chocolate. Scan the heavens from your earthbound vantage point, as wonder and awe fill your heart.

In moments like these your heart is most receptive to God's still, small voice—the voice that comes from within and envelops you with a sense of joy and thankfulness, the voice that tells you that you are more important to him than the moon and all the stars. You are the crowning achievement of all God's creation.

When I consider your heavens,
the work of your fingers,
the moon and the stars,
which you have set in place,
what is man that you are mindful of him,
the son of man that you care for him?
—Psalm 8:3-4

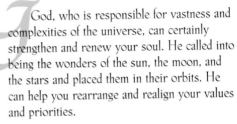

A Moment to Reflect God, who is responsible for vastness and complexities of the universe, can certainly strengthen and renew your soul. He called into being the wonders of the sun, the moon, and the stars and placed them in their orbits. He can help you rearrange and realign your values and priorities.

He created the heavens simply by speaking a word. He can speak words deep inside your soul that can set you free from burdens and cares. You already know that he cares—after all, he's written it in the sky.

To say that God is Creator is another way of
saying that he is Father;
had he not been Father,
he would not have been Creator.
It was being Father that made him want to create.
Because he was infinitely pleased in his Son,
he wanted sons,
and it was in the image of his Son
that he made the world.
His creation was an overflowing
of love and delight.

ॐ

—Louis Evely

The heavens declare the glory of God; and the firmament sheweth his handiwork.

Psalm 19:1 KJV

A Moment to Refresh

This is what the LORD says—
your Redeemer, who formed you in the womb:
I am the LORD, who has made all things,
who alone stretched out the heavens,
who spread out the earth by myself.

Isaiah 44:24

The heavens shall praise thy wonders, O LORD: thy faithfulness also in the congregation of the saints.

Psalm 89:5 KJV

Ever since God created the world, his invisible qualities, both his eternal power and his divine nature, have been clearly seen; they are perceived in the things that God has made.

Romans 1:20 GNT

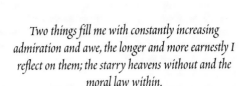

Two things fill me with constantly increasing admiration and awe, the longer and more earnestly I reflect on them; the starry heavens without and the moral law within.

—IMMANUEL KANT

*He who created the heavens,
he is God; he who fashioned
and made the earth, he founded it;
he did not create it to be empty,
but formed it to be inhabited—
he says: "I am the LORD,
and there is no other."*

Isaiah 45:18

*This is what the LORD says...
It is I who made the earth
and created mankind upon it.
My own hands stretched out the heavens;
I marshaled their starry hosts.*

Isaiah 45:11–12

When considering the creation, the how and the when does not matter so much as the why and the wherefore.

—R. DE CAMPOAMOR

A Spot of Tea

For centuries, tea has been the drink of choice for princes and paupers, wise men and fools, aristocrats and commoners. All have treasured it for its calming, relaxing qualities.

Brewing a cup of tea isn't as quick or convenient as popping open a can of soda, but it's worth the small inconvenience. Tea is rich in antioxidants that help to neutralize free radicals, those pesky molecules that can damage cells. A cup of tea has less than half the caffeine of a cup of coffee. Best of all, tea is fat-free, sugar-free, and contains no calories. And oh the variety! It will not be difficult to find one to fit your particular taste—from green and black and oolong tea blends to an impressive selection of herbal or fruity teas, from chamomile to peppermint to peach.

So put on the teapot and retreat from the world for a few glorious minutes. Find a quiet place to relax with a cup of hot freshly brewed tea or a tall glass of iced tea. Sip it slowly, allowing the soothing taste and aroma to comfort you. Let your mind drift freely as you rest and renew yourself.

Take a lesson from tea: its real strength comes out
when it gets into hot water.
——Author Unknown

A Moment to Reflect

God is aware of the complexities and stress-filled circumstances that you face in your life. God cares. He cares so much that he has provided many natural foods that will strengthen and renew body and mind and help you relax and recoup your energy.

When you find yourself feeling the stress, boil the water, steep the tea, and sit for a moment, allowing yourself to enjoy the incredible benefits of a simple cup of tea. These benefits shouldn't be seen as substitutes for the more sophisticated remedies our doctors prescribe for us. But they do represent a wonderful provision for helping us cope successfully in our world. Relax, and know that God created tea for your benefit.

Yellow leaves dance upon the chilly ground
Autumn gusts its last goodbye
To summer sunshine, green, and warmth
While I, cozy inside, put on the kettle and
Ready the table with sweets that delight
And the cup that awaits my ritual of tea.

—TARA AFRIAT

*"I will restore you to health
and heal your wounds,"
declares the LORD.*

Jeremiah 30:17

A Moment to Refresh

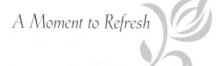

*God causeth the grass to grow for the cattle,
and herb for the service of man.*

Psalm 104:14 KJV

*God blesses the soil which drinks in the rain
that often falls on it and which grows plants that
are useful to those for whom it is cultivated.*

Hebrews 6:7 GNT

*God said, "Behold I have given you every plant
yielding seed that is on the surface of all the
earth, and every tree which has fruit yielding
seed; it shall be food for you."*

Genesis 1:29 NASB

*Whatever you do, whether you eat or drink, do
it all for God's glory.*

1 Corinthians 10:31 GNT

Thank God for tea! What did the world do without tea?
How did it exist? I am glad I was not born before tea.

⟋⟍

—SYDNEY SMITH

Your heart shall rejoice, and your bones
shall flourish like an herb: and the hand of
the LORD *shall be known toward his*
servants.

Isaiah 66:14 KJV

O LORD, *you preserve both man and*
beast....They feast on the abundance
of your house; you give them drink from
your river of delights.

Psalm 36:6, 8

I know that there is nothing better for men
than to be happy and do good while they
live. That everyone may eat and drink, and
find satisfaction in all his toil—this is the
gift of God.

Ecclesiastes 3:12–13

He who has health
has hope, and he
who has hope has
everything.

⟋⟍

—ANCIENT PROVERB

A Song from the Heart

A Moment to Pause Singing has been called the universal cure—all for what ails the soul. The beautiful part is that it doesn't matter how well or how badly a person sings; the remedy works either way.

You may not have the kind of voice that brings fame and fortune, but don't let that stop you. Break out into song, and do it often. Even when you can't physically take a break, give your soul a refreshing interlude by singing a happy song anytime or anyplace you feel comfortable doing so—while driving, while working, while exercising. If you don't know the words, that's not a problem either. Sing along with the radio, make up your own words to a familiar melody, or just hum.

As you sing, let your mind relax. Let the tension and stress in your body flow up and out. Then when you've sung your silly songs and your happy songs, your folk songs and your love songs, sing a song of praise to God for giving you a song to sing and a voice to sing it with.

Let us go singing as far as we go; the road will be less tedious.
—*Virgil A. Kraft*

A Moment to Reflect

When you find yourself in a situation over which you have no reasonable control, sing. God's delightful gift of song was designed for just such a time. It is guaranteed to lift your spirits and chase away the dark shadows of fear and dread. The next time some situation threatens to get you down, try singing "He's Got the Whole World in His Hand" or "What a Friend We Have in Jesus." The gift of song is a remedy for the troubled soul.

Rejoice in the good times and the not-so-bad times, and loosen the occasional tight grip of fear or anxiety with a song. Open your mouth, fill your lungs with air, and burst forth with confidence, joy, and thanksgiving.

O come, let us sing unto the Lord: let us make a joyful noise to the rock of our salvation.
Let us come before his presence with thanksgiving, and make a joyful noise unto him with psalms.
For the Lord is a great God, and a great King above all gods.

—PSALM 95:1-3 KJV

37

Sing and make music in your heart to the Lord.
Ephesians 5:19

A Moment to Refresh

Sing to the LORD a new song,
for he has done marvelous things.

Psalm 98:1

I will sing of your love and justice;
to you, O LORD; I will sing praise.

Psalm 101:1

God put a new song in my mouth,
a song of praise to our God.
Many will see and fear,
and put their trust in the LORD.

Psalm 40:3 NRSV

Miriam took a tambourine in her hand, and all
the women followed her, with tambourines and
dancing. Miriam sang to them: "Sing to the
LORD for he is highly exalted."

Exodus 15:20–21

A careless song, with a little nonsense in it now and then, does not misbecome a monarch.

—HORACE WALPOLE

Serve the LORD with gladness: Come before his presence with singing.
Psalm 100: 2 KJV

*Hear this, you kings! Listen, you rulers!
I will sing to the LORD, I will sing;
I will make music to the LORD,
the God of Israel.*
Judges 5:3

Sing psalms, hymns, and sacred songs; sing to God with thanksgiving in your hearts.
Colossians 3:16 GNT

*By day the LORD directs his love,
at night his song is with me—
a prayer to the God of my life.*
Psalm 42:8

When your heart is full of Christ, you want to sing.

—CHARLES HADDON SPURGEON

The Amazing Bible

A Moment to Pause

Without doubt, the Bible is the most magnificent book ever written. Its words are filled with encouragement and inspiration. Even more than that, the Bible is a living letter from a loving God to you.

It isn't necessary to read a whole book or even a whole chapter at a time. Find a quiet place and a readable version of the Bible. Allow yourself to move about within its pages, soaking up God's promises, gleaning God's wisdom, and learning of God's great love for you. Read each passage twice—once for your head and once for your heart. Go slowly, and allow the richness of God's Word to calm your mind and refresh your soul. Soon you will feel the stress and fatigue of your busy day subsiding.

Try to approach your reading with a fresh mind, and try not to take the meaning of any passage for granted, not to rely only on what you already know. Scripture is so rich with meaning that you can expect new insight and new understanding with each reading. Let God speak to you in new ways.

No matter how much time you spend reading the Bible— even if it is no more than a few minutes a day—you will always be blessed as you read God's life-giving words.

I am sorry for men who do not read the Bible every day.
I wonder why they deprive themselves of the
strength and the pleasure.
—Woodrow Wilson

A Moment to Reflect

By the end of your busy day, you may feel used up and out of resources. Your fatigue is more than just physical tiredness; it permeates your whole being. That's precisely why the Bible is such an extraordinary gift. It has been described as a deep well filled with an endless supply of cool, fresh water.

The time of day you partake of the Bible depends on your personal preferences and needs. The Bible is always there to invigorate, cleanse, and restore you. Find a way to get alone with your Bible for a few minutes each day.

One of the sweet old chapters,
That always will avail,
So full of heavenly comfort,
When earthly comforts fail,
A sweet and blessed message
From God to His children dear,
So rich in precious promises,
So full of love and cheer.

—Author Unknown

Every word of God is pure: he is a shield unto them that put their trust in him.

Proverbs 30:5 KJV

A Moment to Refresh

When your words came, I ate them;
they were my joy and my heart's delight,
O LORD.

Jeremiah 15:16

How sweet are your words to my taste,
O LORD, sweeter than honey
to my mouth!

Psalm 119:103

The precepts of the LORD are right,
giving joy to the heart.

Psalm 19:8

When Moses went and told the people all the
LORD's words and laws, they responded with
one voice, "Everything the LORD has said we
will do." Moses then wrote down everything the
LORD had said.

Exodus 24:3–4

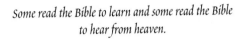

Some read the Bible to learn and some read the Bible to hear from heaven.

ॐ

—Andrew Murray

Jesus said, "It is written, that man shall not live by bread alone, but by every word of God."

Luke 4:4 KJV

The unfolding of your words gives light, O Lord.

Psalm 119:130 NRSV

Jesus said, "If you remain in me and my words remain in you, ask whatever you wish, and it will be given you."

John 15:7

You are my hiding place and my shield, O Lord; I hope in your word.

Psalm 119:114 NRSV

I have found in the Bible words for my inmost thoughts, songs for my joy, utterance for my hidden griefs and pleadings for my shame and feebleness.

ॐ

—Samuel Taylor Coleridge

Picture This

Memories are precious. Even those stored during bad times contain the lacy crystals of hope and joy, and they remind you of God's tender hand encouraging and delivering you in your time of need. Other memories remind you of good times with images you want to keep forever—a loved one's smile, children as they grow, places you've been, and people you've known.

Take a break from the busyness of your day and immerse yourself in your precious memories. Find a quiet place and walk through the family picture album, or the photographs you took on that great vacation a few years ago. Let the rich memories envelop and draw you back to another place and time. Move slowly; give yourself time to match your memory with the photograph.

As you move along your trail of memories, whisper a word of thanksgiving to God for each person and place God has used to decorate your life. Laugh and cry, smile and sigh as you wander through. The release of your emotions will help your tension dissipate and restore to you a sense of happiness and well-being.

God gave us memory so that we might have
roses in December.
—James M. Barrie

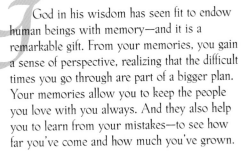

God in his wisdom has seen fit to endow human beings with memory—and it is a remarkable gift. From your memories, you gain a sense of perspective, realizing that the difficult times you go through are part of a bigger plan. Your memories allow you to keep the people you love with you always. And they also help you to learn from your mistakes—to see how far you've come and how much you've grown.

As you take your walk down memory lane, let God show you how, by his grace, you have made a difference and have received a bounty of gifts from his hands.

What a strange thing is memory, and hope;
One looks backward, the other forward.
The one is of today, the other is the tomorrow.
Memory is history recorded in our brain,
memory is a painter, it paints pictures
of the past and of the day.

—Grandma Moses

The memory of the righteous will be a blessing.
Proverbs 10:7

A Moment to Refresh

One generation shall praise thy works to
another, and shall declare thy mighty acts, O
LORD.... They shall abundantly utter the
memory of thy great goodness, and shall sing of
thy righteousness.

Psalm 145:4, 7 KJV

God has caused his wonders to be remembered;
the LORD is gracious and compassionate.

Psalm 111:4

Look to the LORD and his strength;
seek his face always.
Remember the wonders he has done,
his miracles, and the judgments he pronounced.

Psalm 105:4–5

The beauty of memory is that it still sees beauty when beauty has faded.

—Paul Boese

I will remember the years of the right hand of the most High. I will remember the works of the Lord: surely I will remember thy wonders of old.

Psalm 77:10-11 KJV

A righteous man will be remembered forever.

Psalm 112:6

Sing unto the Lord, O ye saints of his, and give thanks at the remembrance of his holiness.

Psalm 30:4 KJV

Jesus said, "The Comforter, which is the Holy Ghost, whom the Father will send in my name, he shall teach you all things, and bring all things to your remembrance, whatsoever I have said unto you."

John 14:26 KJV

Memory tempers prosperity, mitigates adversity, controls youth, and delights old age.

—Author Unknown

Considering a Tree

A Moment to Pause Like people and snowflakes, every tree is unique—each is truly a one-of-a-kind creation. Perhaps that's why a tree never fails to inspire a sense of wonder when one stops to take a closer look.

In the midst of your busy day, take a few minutes to ponder the magnificence of a tree that lives and grows near you. Slowly run your hand along its trunk. Is the bark smooth and a little sticky, made up of hard lumpy squares, or something in between? Take one of its leaves and trace its lines and ridges with your fingertips. Step back and gaze up into the branches, noting the way they have been shaped and turned by the wind and rain. Imagine the roots burrowing underground, providing stability, strength, and nourishment.

As you do this, consider the fact that you are God's unique creation. Like the tree, you are one of a kind, molded and shaped by the hand of God. Let that understanding lift your spirit and refresh your soul. Then open your heart and whisper a greeting to God, who uses even a tree to remind you of his great love for you.

Poems are made by fools like me,
but only God can make a tree.
——Joyce Kilmer

A Moment to Reflect

God created all the wonders we see in the natural world. When he was finished, he looked it over and said that it was good. Then he created man and woman. God created mankind, unlike trees and other elements of his creation, in his very own image. He invested in each person a singular combination of God likeness.

If your busy lifestyle has left you feeling lost in the crowd, slow down for a few minutes to consider the distinctive beauty of a tree. Then remind yourself that you, created in his image, are the crown of God's creation.

Tossed on a windy sea
the great oak surrenders
its last brittle browning leaves
to the silent ground below—
Still she stands—arms upraised—
to sing the psalm of seasons,
of God's eternal praise.

TARA AFRIAT

You will go out in joy and be led forth in peace; the mountains and hills will burst into song before you, and all the trees of the field will clap their hands.

Isaiah 55:12

A Moment to Refresh

Happy are those who... find joy in obeying the Law of the LORD, and they study it day and night. They are like trees that grow beside a stream, that bear fruit at the right time, and whose leaves do not dry up. They succeed in everything they do.

Psalm 1:1–3 GNT

They will be called oaks of righteousness, a planting of the LORD for the display of his splendor.

Isaiah 61:3

I am like an olive tree flourishing in the house of God; I trust in God's unfailing love for ever and ever.

Psalm 52:8

No town can fail of beauty, though its walks were gutters and its houses hovels, if venerable trees make magnificent colonnades along its street.

✽

—Henry Ward Beecher

The fruit of the righteous is a tree of life.
Proverbs 11:30

To him who overcomes, Jesus will give the right to eat from the tree of life, which is in the paradise of God.
Revelation 2:7

Know that the LORD is God. It is he who made us, and we are his; we are his people, the sheep of his pasture.
Psalm 100:3

The righteous will flourish like a palm tree, they will grow like a cedar of Lebanon.
Psalm 92:12

A woodland in full color is awesome as a forest fire, in magnitude at least; but a single tree is like a dancing tongue of flame to warm the heart.

✽

—Hal Borland

Sweet Sleep

A Moment to Pause

A power nap in the early afternoon refreshes the body and stimulates creativity. Remember when grade-school teachers told their students to put their heads down on their desks for a few minutes of quiet and rest? A little nap was good for the teacher as well.

Try closing your office door and putting your head down on your desk for a few minutes. If you're at home, curl up on the sofa or flip back in the recliner. Close your eyes and consciously relax one part of your body at a time until you drift off into the warm cocoon of sleep. Let yourself remain in the arms of slumber for ten to fifteen minutes before rousing yourself to go on with your day.

You will feel energized, refreshed, and renewed. Work will seem easier and more enjoyable. Ideas will come more easily. Obstacles will seem less intimidating. God has given you sweet rest—a delightful way to recharge your mind and body.

I found I could add nearly two hours to my working day
by going to bed for an hour after luncheon.
—Sir Winston Churchill

A Moment to Reflect

Your body is an amazing machine, designed to run with great efficiency. In most cases, it will keep right on moving as long as you want it to, but how much better it functions when you stop for a few minutes to rest. Rest is a natural prescription for well-being and productivity.

When your hectic life leaves you feeling dull and uninspired, try a nap. If you aren't able to fall asleep, just lean back, close your eyes, and rest for a few minutes. When you feel refreshed, thank God for knowing exactly what you need and for the remarkable resilience of the body he has given you.

When, spurred by tasks unceasing or undone,
You would seek rest afar,
And cannot, though repose be rightly won—
Rest where you are.

Neglect the needless; sanctify the rest;
Move without stress or jar;
With quiet of a spirit self-possessed.
Rest where you are.

—Author Unknown

Jesus said, "Come to me, all you who are weary and burdened, and I will give you rest. Take my yoke upon you and learn from me, for I am gentle and humble in heart, and you will find rest for your souls."

Matthew 11:28–29

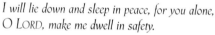

A Moment to Refresh

I will lie down and sleep in peace, for you alone, O LORD, make me dwell in safety.

Psalm 4:8

On my bed I remember you; I think of you through the watches of the night. Because you are my help, I sing in the watches of the night. Because you are my help, I sing in the shadow of your wings.

Psalm 62:6–7

Keep sound wisdom and discretion.... When you lie down, you will not be afraid; When you lie down, your sleep will be sweet.

Proverbs 3:21, 24 NASB

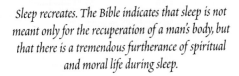

Sleep recreates. The Bible indicates that sleep is not meant only for the recuperation of a man's body, but that there is a tremendous furtherance of spiritual and moral life during sleep.

—OSWALD CHAMBERS

The sleep of a laborer is sweet, whether he eats little or much.

Ecclesiastes 5:12

The LORD is my shepherd.... He lets me rest in fields of green grass and leads me to quiet pools of fresh water. He gives me new strength.

Psalm 23:1–3 GNT

My soul finds rest in God alone; my salvation comes from him.

Psalm 62:1

I lie down and sleep; I wake again, because the LORD sustains me.

Psalm 3:5

Those whose spirits are stirred by the breath of the Holy Spirit go forward even in sleep.

—BROTHER ANDREW

A Poet's Heart

A Moment to Pause

The poet's ready pen graces the reader with beauty, laughter, romance, and much more. There would seem to be no end to the combinations of words and thoughts and emotion that poetry lays out—timeless gifts strewn at your feet.

Wrap yourself up in a poem. Find several that you really like and spend a few minutes reading them, soaking up the emotions of love and joy and sorrow and triumph they provide. Read them slowly, taking in each word, tuning into the rhythms and rhymes. Soon you'll sense them dancing along the edges of your mind, urging you to come out and play awhile, happy and carefree.

And if you begin to hear your own rhythms and rhymes during your poetry breaks, don't hesitate to exercise your creative juices. It won't be long before your soul will be spilling over with inspiration applicable to many other areas of your life. When it comes, roll with it; allow it to become part of you, providing a delightful outlet for all the feelings that follow you through your busy life.

Poetry is the language in which man explores his own amazement.
—Christopher Fry

A Moment to Reflect

Emotions like joy, happiness, love, and courage can be so strong that they well up within you, struggling to find an outlet of expression. Poetry is a wonderful way to vent those feelings. Somehow the rhythms and rhymes loosen the tongue and allow one to verbalize more easily.

Whether you are reading poetry or writing it, open your heart and ask God to help you express all that your heart longs to say. Then let your mind and soul revel in the beauty and inspiration of the verse. Grab on and let it pull you along, ushering you into a world of enchantment.

The poet's eye, in a fine frenzy rolling,
Doth glance from heaven to earth,
from earth to heaven;
And as imagination bodies forth
the forms of things unknown,
The poet's pen turns them to shapes,
and gives to airy nothing
a local habitation and a name.

—WILLIAM SHAKESPEARE

LORD, you are like a shield that keeps me safe.
You help me win the battle. Your strong right
hand keeps me going. You bend down to make
me great.

Psalm 18:35 NIV

A Moment to Refresh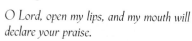

O Lord, open my lips, and my mouth will
declare your praise.

Psalm 51:15

Sing to the LORD a new song, for he has done
marvelous thing.... Shout for joy to the Lord, all
the earth, burst into jubilant song with music.

Psalm 98:1, 4

"The good man brings good things out of the
good stored up in his heart.... For out of the
overflow of his heart his mouth speaks."

Luke 6:45

Beautiful words fill my mind, as I compose this
song for the king. Like the pen of a good writer
my tongue is ready with a poem.

Psalm 45:1 GNT

*Poetry is the spontaneous overflow of powerful feelings:
it takes its origin from emotion recollected in tranquility.*

—WILLIAM WORDSWORTH

*Sing to the LORD a new song; play
skillfully, and shout for joy.*

Psalm 33:3

*Trust in him at all times, O people; pour
out your hearts to him, for God is our
refuge.*

Psalm 62:8

*I will sing a new song to you, O God;
on the ten-stringed lyre I will make music
to you.*

Psalm 144:9

*I—to the LORD, I will sing, I will sing
praise to the LORD.*

Judges 5:3 NASB

*The poet speaks to
all men of that other
life of theirs that
they have smothered
and forgotten.*

—*DAME EDITH
SITWELL*

The Sound of Music

A Moment to Pause

Ah, the sweet sound of music. Since the beginning, it has soothed, calmed, inspired, and lifted souls. The experience of music has an uncanny way of evoking deep emotions—joy, sadness, tenderness, courage, love, compassion. Music brings feelings to the surface and makes one feel alive and vital.

Give your soul a treat by switching on your radio or sound system and losing yourself for a few wonderful moments in crisp beats and rich melodies. Let them wash over you again and again, pulling you in and touching your heart. Listen to the words. Think about them. Then hum or sing along. Let the music flood your soul until you feel it nourishing you from the inside out.

Choose a style of music that connects with you on the inside. Sit back and relax while you listen, letting the sounds whisk you away from cares and obligations. Or get up on your feet and dance. Close your eyes and move your arms and legs, choreographing your own unique dance. You'll soon find yourself happy and relaxed, refreshed in a whole new way.

Music washes away from the soul the dust of everyday life.
—Berthold Auerbach

A Moment to Reflect

Music is one of God's most gracious gifts. It can help you to connect with him in a very special way, to lose yourself in worship, praise, and adoration. Music can help you to transcend your inhibitions and move to a new level of openness.

Whether you are listening to a symphony, a hymn, or pop tunes, let the music lift you and renew you. Sing a song of praise to God for the delightful and diverse gift of music he has placed in your life. If you listen carefully, you might even hear him singing along with you.

Yes, music is the prophet's art;
Among the gifts that God hath sent,
One of the most magnificent!
It calms the agitated heart;
Temptations, evil thoughts, and all
The passions that disturb the soul,
Are quelled by its divine control,
As the evil spirit fled from Saul,
And his distemper was allayed,
When David took his harp and played.

—Henry Wadsworth Longfellow

It is good to praise the Lord and make music to your name, O Most High.

Psalm 92:1

A Moment to Refresh

Whenever the spirit from God came upon Saul, David would take his harp and play. Then relief would come to Saul; he would feel better.

1 Samuel 16:23

Moses and the Israelites sang this song to the Lord:... "The Lord is my strength and my song; he has become my salvation. He is my God, and I will praise him, my father's God, and I will exalt him."

Exodus 15:1–2

The music of the strings makes the LORD glad.

Psalm 45:8

Let us come before the LORD with thanksgiving and extol him with music and song.

Psalm 95:2

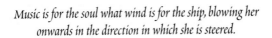

Music is for the soul what wind is for the ship, blowing her onwards in the direction in which she is steered.

— WILLIAM BOOTH

I will sing and make music.... I will praise you, O LORD, among the nations; I will sing of you among the peoples. For great is your love, reaching to the heavens; your faithfulness reaches to the skies.
Psalm 57:7, 9–10

The LORD your God is with you, he is mighty to save. He will take great delight in you, he will quiet you with his love, he will rejoice over you with singing.
Zephaniah 3:17

LORD, you are my hiding place; you will protect me from trouble and surround me with songs of deliverance.
Psalm 32:7

Music exalts each joy, allays each grief. Expels diseases, softens every pain.

—JOHN ARMSTRONG

Time for Two Wheels

A Moment to Pause

Fast is good! But not-quite-so-fast might be even better when it comes to the soul. So before you start up the engine on your four-wheel transportation, look around the garage and see if there isn't an adventurous two-wheel alternative awaiting.

One doesn't have to cycle across Nova Scotia to enjoy the thrill. The sights, the sounds, the sun on your face, the breeze moving through your hair—those are the things you notice when you ride a bike. Once or twice around the block can be a wonderful break. As you climb astride, take a deep breath. Allow yourself to focus on the motion, the up and down of your legs on the pedals, the rubber grips and cool metal of the handlebars.

Take time to glide along and to reacquaint yourself with the neighborhood. Take time to notice the trees, the yards, the people. Take time to notice what's new and what's not. Take the opportunity to reconnect with the world you live in. Then give thanks for what you see around you—the wonder of a squirrel racing up a tree, a dog barking in a yard, children at play. Thank him for strong lungs and strong legs and two wheels to carry you along.

Energy is the power that drives every human being.
It is not lost by exertion but maintained by it.
—Germaine Greer

A Moment to Reflect

Your busy lifestyle requires quick, reliable, weatherproof transportation. But, oh, what wonders you can enjoy when you pay attention to the journey as much as to the destination.

God has created all the beauty of this world for you. Slowing down and taking note is an amazing way to gain perspective and give your soul a break from the drudgery of routine. Hopping on a bike can free you for a few precious moments from the mundane and reacquaint you with the magic of fresh air and the joy of freewheeling on the way to nowhere in particular.

As I pass quickly through my day
I never seem to look about
And see the flowers
You've laid out

Lord, touch my heart
And help me see
The world that you have
Made for me.

—ROBERTA S. CULLEY

65

The earth is the LORD's, and everything in it,
the world, and all who live in it.

Psalm 24:1

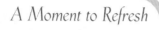

A Moment to Refresh

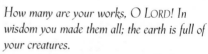

How many are your works, O LORD! In
wisdom you made them all; the earth is full of
your creatures.

Psalm 104:24

Physical exercise has some value, but spiritual
exercise is valuable in every way, because it
promises life both for the present and for the
future.

1 Timothy 4:8 GNT

The heavens proclaim his righteousness, and all
the peoples see his glory.

Psalm 97:6

Love the LORD your God with all your heart
and with all your soul and with all your
strength.

Deuteronomy 6:5

To travel hopefully is a better thing than to arrive, and the true success is to labor.

∾

—ROBERT LOUIS STEVENSON

Whatever is true, whatever is noble,
whatever is right, whatever is pure,
whatever is lovely, whatever is admirable—
if anything is excellent or praiseworthy—
think about such things.

Philippians 4:8

Happy are those who find wisdom, and
those who get understanding.... Her ways
are ways of pleasantness, and all her paths
are peace.

Proverbs 3:13, 17 NRSV

They that wait upon the Lord shall renew
their strength; they shall mount up with
wings as eagles; they shall run, and not be
weary; and they shall walk, and not faint.

Isaiah 40:31 KJV

Every one has time
if he likes. Business
runs after nobody:
people cling to it of
their own free will
and think that to be
busy is a proof of
happiness.

∾

—SENECA

The Voice of a Friend

A Moment to Pause

What a blessing friendship is. The comfort of a touch, a smile, a knowing look, a familiar voice. Your friends know you, and you feel safe with them—safe to call for no reason, to speak your mind, to unload your bundle of irritations, to share a humorous moment. With a friend there is rest and comfort and acceptance for your soul.

Close your eyes for a moment and let the faces of your friends flow through your mind. Then choose one that fits your mood. If you're feeling a little down, choose someone who has a knack for cheering you up. If you are feeling insecure, choose someone who is good at making you feel that you are okay. If you just want a social moment, call someone with whom you enjoy sharing your thoughts. It may have been awhile since you spoke to that person, but don't let that keep you from punching in the number.

Once you get your friend on the line, don't rush. Soak up each word of encouragement, opportunity to laugh, and sympathetic response. It will do your soul good like a medicine. It isn't necessary to talk for hours—just checking in will provide refreshment for both of you.

Friendship is a sheltering tree.
—Author Unknown

God created humans with a deep longing for fellowship. It is what draws us to relationship with him. And it is what reminds us that we need each other. What a glorious gift we have been given.

The next time your soul longs for fellowship, pick up the phone. Make a connection with a friend, chat for a few minutes, exchange news. Let the sound of your friend's voice give you the connection that your spirit craves. If your friend doesn't answer, call on God. Your call will never go unanswered. He's always at home and always ready to listen...he's the best friend of all.

Oh, the comfort, the inexpressible comfort of feeling safe with a person, having neither to weigh thoughts nor measure words, but pouring them all out, just as they are, chaff and grain together, certain that a faithful hand will take and sift them, keep what is worth keeping, and with a breath of kindness blow the rest away.

—DINAH MARIA MULOCK CRAIK

*A man of many companions may come to ruin,
but there is a friend who sticks closer than a
brother.*

Proverbs 18:24

A Moment to Refresh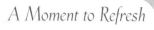

A friend loves at all times.

Proverbs 17:17

*Two are better than one, because they have a
good return for their work: If one falls down,
his friend can help him up.*

Ecclesiastes 4:9–10

*Iron sharpens iron, and one person sharpens
the wits of another.*

Proverbs 27:17 NRSV

*God is faithful; by him you were called into the
fellowship of his Son, Jesus Christ our Lord.*

1 Corinthians 1:9 NRSV

*Jonathan said to David, "Go in peace, for we
have sworn friendship with each other in the
name of the LORD.*

1 Samuel 20:42

A friend is a present you give yourself.

—AUTHOR UNKNOWN

Jesus said, "I no longer call you servants,
because a servant does not know his
master's business. Instead, I have called
you friends, for everything that I learned
from my Father I have made known to you.
John 15:15

Jesus said, "Here I am! I stand at the door
and knock. If anyone hears my voice and
opens the door, I will come in and eat with
him, and he with me."
Revelation 3:20

My friends, how dear you are to me and
how I miss you! How happy you make me,
and how proud I am of you!... It is a great
joy to me that after so long a time you once
more had the chance of showing that you
care for me.
Philippians 4:1, 10 GNT

*A true friend
unbosoms freely,
advises justly, assists
readily, adventures
boldly, takes all
patiently, defends
courageously, and
continues a friend
unchangeably.*

—WILLIAM PENN

Stop to Smell the Flowers

Flowers serve as God's flamboyant designer touches: grand, robust chrysanthemums; full, creamy—soft roses; happy, yellow—and—brown daisies; dazzling bluebonnets pointing to the sky. God has placed an enormous assortment of beauty across the face of the earth. And all that amazing medley of colors, smells, and textures is yours to enjoy.

One day soon, as you're walking to your office building, unloading the groceries from the van, walking to the mailbox, or doing whatever your particular routine asks of you, slow down and take a close look at what God has done. You are apt to see a kaleidoscope of flowery grandeur. Even dandelions in the grass are a visual feast. And you may think winter has nothing to offer, but for the watchful eye, it affords a rich variety of evergreen shrubs with colorful berries.

Let your eyes devour the beauty and each startling detail of God's flora. Run your fingers over the petals, delighting in the delicate touch. Then, take a deep breath, drawing in the fragrances. Even on gloomy days, flowers have a way of capturing one's soul and filling it with sunshine.

Don't hurry, don't worry.
You're only here for a short visit. So be sure to
stop and smell the flowers.
—Walter C. Hagen

So much is expected of you each day. No wonder you rush about with a long list of tasks to accomplish and responsibilities to take care of. That may be why God has strewn such magnificent beauty in your path—to enrich your soul as you rush by.

Open your eyes to it all—the flowering trees and shrubs that decorate the landscapes of your world. Take time to delight in the blossoming gardens and fields of wild flowers that come your way. From there, your soul will find its own rest in the remarkable scope of God's creative genius.

I remember, I remember
The roses, red and white,
The violets, and the lily-cups,
Those flowers made of light!
The lilacs, where the robin built,
And where my brother set
The laburnum on his birthday—
The tree is living yet.

—HOOD

73

*By Christ all things were created: things in
heaven and on earth, visible and invisible...
all things were created by him and for him.*

Colossians 1:16

A Moment to Refresh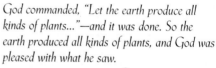

*God commanded, "Let the earth produce all
kinds of plants..."—and it was done. So the
earth produced all kinds of plants, and God was
pleased with what he saw.*

Genesis 1:11–12 GNT

*Flowers appear on the earth;
the season of singing has come,
the cooing of doves is heard in our land.
The fig tree forms its early fruit;
the blossoming vines spread their fragrance.*

Song of Solomon 2:12–13

*The desert and the parched land will be glad;
the wilderness will rejoice and blossom.
Like the crocus, it will burst into bloom;
it will rejoice greatly and shout for joy.*

Isaiah 35:1-2

The flower is the poetry of reproduction. It is an example of the eternal seductiveness of life.

—JEAN GIRAUDOUX

Jesus said, "Consider how the lilies grow. They do not labor or spin. Yet I tell you, not even Solomon in all his splendor was dressed like one of these."

Luke 12:27

As for man, his days are like grass, he flourishes like a flower of the field.

Psalm 103:15

The grass withers and the flowers fall, but the word of our God stands forever.

Isaiah 40:8

Let us go early to the vineyards to see if the vines have budded, if their blossoms have opened, and if the pomegranates are in bloom.

Song of Solomon 7:12

Flowers are the sweetest things that God ever made, and forgot to put a soul into.

—HENRY WARD BEECHER

The Love of God

Just as food provides fuel for the body, God's love provides fuel for the soul. Not only does it sustain one's innermost being, but it literally gives it life. Focusing your mind on the miracle of grace brings refreshment, renewal, and rest to your soul.

Wherever you are, whatever you're doing, focus your mind on God and meditate on the fact that he chose to love you before you even knew him. Think about how extraordinary it is that he gave you a free will, endowing you with the right to receive his love freely and without coercion.

As you think about these things, bask in the sunshine of God's commitment to you, his love for you, his confidence in you. Feel it as it warms you from the outside in. Allow God's love to well up from the inside, strengthening and inspiring you.

As you go on with the affairs of your day, hold God's love close to your heart. Draw on it for courage and encouragement. Feast on it for nourishment and sustenance. Cherish it, and it will bring life and health to your soul.

In his love he clothes us, enfolds us and embraces us;
that tender love completely surrounds us, never to leave us.
—Julian of Norwich

A Moment to Reflect

God's love is a life-giving force, a treasure beyond comprehension. When you open your heart to it, it warms and feeds your soul, and from you it travels outward to others. God's love is intangible, yet your whole self fuels, connects, responds, and shares His love intuitively and instinctively.

The God who created the universe has chosen to pour out his love on you. In his sovereignty and wisdom, he chose to do so. What greater gift could ever be given? What greater understanding could more surely restore your soul?

Jesu, lover of my soul,
Let me to thy bosom fly,
While the nearer waters roll,
While the tempest still is high;
Hide me, O my Savior, hide,
Till the storm of life is past;
Safe into the haven glide
O receive my soul at last.

—CHARLES WESLEY

Give thanks to the LORD, for he is good.
His love endures forever.

Psalm 136:1

A Moment to Refresh

God so loved the world that he gave his one and
only Son, that whoever believes in him shall not
perish but have eternal life.

John 3:16

As high as the heavens are above the earth,
so great is God's love for those who fear him.

Psalm 103:11

God chose us in Christ before the creation of
the world.

Ephesians 1:4

Let us love one another, for love comes from
God. Everyone who loves has been born of God
and knows God.

1 John 4:7

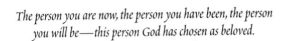

The person you are now, the person you have been, the person you will be—this person God has chosen as beloved.

ॐ

—WILLIAM COUNTRYMAN

I pray that you, being rooted and established in love, may have power, together with all the saints, to grasp how wide and long and high and deep is the love of Christ, and to know this love that surpasses knowledge—that you may be filled to the measure of all the fullness of God.

Ephesians 3:17–19

Jesus said, "You did not choose me, but I chose you and appointed you to go and bear fruit—fruit that will last."

John 15:16

God demonstrates his own love for us in this: While we were still sinners, Christ died for us.

Romans 5:8

All God can give us is his love, and this love becomes tangible—a burning of the soul—it sets us on fire to the point of forgetting ourselves.

ॐ

—BROTHER ROGER

Over the Back Fence

A Moment to Pause

Conversation is the cornerstone of relationship and the facilitator of fellowship. It is the means by which one soul connects with another. Engaging in conversation can be a wonderful respite for the inner person, providing both stimulation and inspiration.

Give your soul a welcome break by chatting with a neighbor over the back fence, the person packing your groceries, another patient in the waiting room, a stranger in the elevator, one of your children, or your spouse. No need to get deep and serious. Even topics like the weather and current events can fuel interesting, upbeat conversations. The interaction is more important than the topic.

As you converse, shoo away interrupting thoughts, inhibitions, or shyness. Concentrate on the person you are speaking with. Ask open questions and listen carefully to the answers. Allow yourself to respond emotionally to what you're hearing and saying. Laugh, tell jokes, show compassion. Soon you will feel yourself relaxing and gaining new perspective on life.

Don't worry about who is doing the most talking. It's fun to lose yourself in someone else's story. Not only will your moments of conversation serve to refresh your mind and soul, but they will almost certainly do the same for the other person.

Do you know that conversation is one of the greatest pleasures in life? But it wants leisure.
—W. Somerset Maugham

A Moment to Reflect

God always meant for people to know one another, care for one another, and love one another. Conversation breaks down walls and creates bridges from person to person, soul to soul.

There may be days when you feel the need to let a warm, refreshing breeze blow through your soul. When that happens, open your mouth and reach out to someone in the form of conversation. You will sense your walls coming down and your heart rising up. It's a delightful way to invest your time and bless two lives in the process.

Talk with us, Lord, Thyself reveal,
While there o'er earth we move;
Speak to our hearts, and let us feel
The kindling of Thy love.

With Thee conversing, we forget
All time, and toil, and care;
Labor is rest, and pain is sweet,
If Thou, my God, art here.

—CHARLES WESLEY

A man that hath friends must show himself friendly.

Proverbs 18:24 KJV

A Moment to Refresh

Greet all the saints in Christ Jesus.

Philippians 4:21

Greet all your leaders and all God's people.

Hebrews 13:24

Jesus said, "Where two or three come together in my name, there am I with them."

Matthew 18:20

Jesus said, "A new command I give you: Love one another. As I have loved you, so you must love one another."

John 13:34

I have much to write to you, but I do not want to use paper and ink. Instead, I hope to visit you and talk with you face to face, so that our joy may be complete.

2 John 1:12

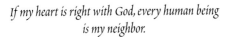

If my heart is right with God, every human being is my neighbor.

—OSWALD CHAMBERS

Everyone should be quick to listen.
James 1:19

May the grace of the Lord Jesus Christ, and the love of God, and the fellowship of the Holy Spirit be with you all.
2 Corinthians 13:14

If we walk in the light, as he is in the light, we have fellowship with one another.
1 John 1:7

Those who revered the LORD spoke with one another. The LORD took note and listened, and a book of rememberance was written before him of those who revered the LORD and thought on his name.
Malachi 3:16 NRSV

While the spirit of neighborliness was important on the frontier because neighbors were so few, it is even more important now because our neighbors are so many.

—LADY BIRD JOHNSON

Just Plant It

Mud pies aren't about eating; they are all about digging in the dirt and feeling the dark, rich soil flow. The instinct to do so has been handed down from the first gardener—Adam.

You may not be itching to wallow in the mud, but take a few minutes to dig a little hole and plant something. Don't panic if you don't have a green thumb. It isn't necessary to put in an entire vegetable garden or to landscape your yard. Gardening can be as simple as planting one small flowerpot.

Once you've decided what to plant where, just dig in. Using a spade, turn the soil, letting your senses take in the experience. Notice the texture and color of the soil. Is it light and sandy or dark and rich? Focus next on the wonderful fragrance. Close your eyes and let your sense of smell take over. Then scoop out a place for the seeds or seedlings. While you work, imagine God planting you in the nourishing soil of his love. Put the plant in place and pack in the soil around it. Then water it gently, reminding yourself of the tender way God waters your soul.

God Almighty first planted a garden; and indeed,
it is the purest of human pleasures.
——Francis Bacon

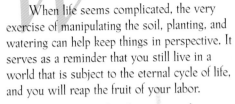

A Moment to Reflect

When life seems complicated, the very exercise of manipulating the soil, planting, and watering can help keep things in perspective. It serves as a reminder that you still live in a world that is subject to the eternal cycle of life, and you will reap the fruit of your labor.

Working the soil and watching a living thing thrive and grow will help you reclaim your sense of purpose and your personal worth—reestablishing your belief that life is worth living and your dreams are attainable. Digging in the dirt is an exercise in faith, hope, and love.

Oh, Adam was a gardener, and God
who made him sees
That half a proper gardener's work is
done upon his knees,
So when your work is finished,
You can wash your hands and pray
For the Glory of the Garden, that it
may not pass away!

—RUDYARD KIPLING

The LORD God took the man and put him in
the Garden of Eden to work it and take care of
it.

Genesis 2:15

A Moment to Refresh

The LORD God had planted a garden in the
east, in Eden; and... made all kinds of trees
grow out of the ground—trees that were
pleasing to the eye and good for food.

Genesis 2:8–9

Jesus said, "A man scatters seed on the ground.
Night and day, whether he sleeps or gets up, the
seed sprouts and grows, though he does not
know how. All by itself the soil produces
grain—first the stalk, then the head, then the full
kernel in the head."

Mark 4:26–28

Jesus said, "What shall we say the kingdom of
God is like, or what parable shall we use to
describe it? It is like a mustard seed, which is
the smallest seed you plant in the ground. Yet
when planted, it grows and becomes the largest
of all garden plants, with such big branches that
the birds of the air can perch in its shade."

Mark 4:30–32

To own a bit of ground, to scratch it with a hoe, to plant seeds, and watch their renewal of life—this is the commonest delight of the race, the most satisfactory thing a man can do.

—CHARLES DUDLEY WARNER

Jesus said, "The seed on good soil stands for those with a noble and good heart, who hear the word, retain it, and by persevering produce a crop."

Luke 8:15

I delight greatly in the Lord; my soul rejoices in my God.... As the soil makes the sprout come up and a garden causes seeds to grow, so the Sovereign LORD will make righteousness and praise spring up before all nations.

Isaiah 61:10–11

Because Uzziah loved farming, he encouraged the people to plant vineyards in the hill country and to farm the fertile land.

1 Corinthians 26:10 GNT

The kiss of sun for pardon,
The song of the birds for mirth
One is nearer God's Heart in a garden
Than anywhere else on earth.

—DOROTHY GURNEY

Peaceful Pets

A Moment to Pause

Pets may chirp, bark, meow, oink, or swim quietly. Pets bring love, loyalty, laughs, and other wonderful things to one's life. They provide companionship and spark contentment.

If you have a pet in your life, take a few minutes from your busy day and enjoy what God has given you. Talk up a storm— pets are great listeners, and they never give away your secrets. But do more than talking. Take a little vacation into your pet's world. Lay by the fire with your dog, slouch on the sofa with your cat, perch on a chair near your bird's cage. Then let your pet lead the way, initiating affection and play. Making a solid connection with another living thing can be delightful.

If you don't have a pet, animals can still provide a retreat for your soul. Hang a bird feeder outside your window, visit a pond and feed the ducks and geese, or take a few minutes to watch the squirrels racing around the backyard.

Animals are such agreeable friends—they ask no questions, they pass no criticisms.
——George Eliot

A Moment to Reflect

God meant for animals to enrich your life. As you spend time with your pet, allow yourself to soak up the warmth and rest in it. Take time to thank God for caring so much about you that he created more than the beauty of the mountains and the oceans and the sky. As an expression of his creative genius, he has also given you living things.

Enjoy the living gift that God has given you. Let the birds and the fish and the beasts encourage, refresh, and comfort your soul, just as God intended.

Wolves and sheep will live together in peace,
and leapards will lie down with young goats.
Calves and lion cubs will feed together,
and little children will take care of them.
Cows and bears will eat together,
and their calves and cubs will lie down in peace.
Lions will eat straw as cattle do.
Even a baby will not be harmed
if it plays near a poisonous snake.
On Zion, God's sacred hill,
there will be nothing harmful or evil.

—ISAIAH 11:6–9

God made the wild animals according to their kinds, the livestock according to their kinds, and all the creatures that move along the ground according to their kinds. And God saw that it was good.

Genesis 1:25

A Moment to Refresh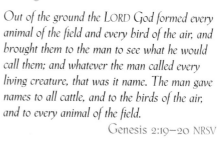

Out of the ground the LORD God formed every animal of the field and every bird of the air, and brought them to the man to see what he would call them; and whatever the man called every living creature, that was it name. The man gave names to all cattle, and to the birds of the air, and to every animal of the field.

Genesis 2:19–20 NRSV

All kinds of animals, birds, reptiles and creatures of the sea are being tamed and have been tamed by man.

James 3:7

The birds of the air nest by the waters; they sing among the branches.

Psalm 104:12

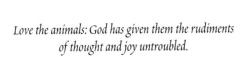

Love the animals: God has given them the rudiments of thought and joy untroubled.

—FYODER DOSTOEVSKY

My mouth will speak in praise of the Lord. Let every creature praise his holy name for ever and ever.

Psalm 145:21

God... richly provides us with everything for our enjoyment.

1 Timothy 6:17

Jesus said, "Consider the ravens: They do not sow or reap, they have no storeroom or barn; yet God feeds them. And how much more valuable you are than birds!"

Luke 12:24

God gave Solomon very great wisdom, discernment, and breadth of understanding.... He would speak of animals, and birds, and reptiles, and fish.

1 Kings 4:29, 33 NRSV

The great pleasure of a dog is that you may make a fool of yourself with him and not only will he not scold you, but he will make a fool of himself too.

—SAMUEL BUTLER

Thank You

A Moment to Pause

Day by day, week by week, people pass through your life, touching you with wisdom, encouragement, and hope. Some bring physical blessings, some give glimpses into the meaning of life, and others bring laughter and optimism.

Take a few minutes to remind yourself of the people God has sent into your life and the wonderful blessings they have brought your way. Then find paper and a pen on which to write a thank-you note. Before you begin, sit back and focus on the person to whom you are writing and meditate on what he or she has meant to you. Picture the person in your mind and allow your thoughts and emotions to carry you where they want to go. Even if you no longer know how to reach the person, or even if he or she is no longer living, writing that note can be a wonderful, soul-enriching experience.

When you're ready to write, let your feelings flow freely. Don't worry about using the right words, just speak from your heart. The very act of writing out your thank-you affirms both the giver and the receiver, and it reestablishes those special words and actions that so blessed you in the past.

Thanksgiving is good but thanks-living is better.
—*Matthew Henry*

A Moment to Reflect

Exercising thankfulness feels like an adrenaline rush for the soul. It's a great way to lift your spirits on a not-so-happy day or to feel the warmth of sunshine when the weather is cold and dreary. And when one acknowledges the blessing, God blesses again.

Thanking those whose lives have touched yours can boost your self-esteem and inspire you in your relationships with others, motivating you to pass the wisdom and encouragement and hope along. What a marvelous way to honor those who have given of themselves to you while, at the same time, to refresh your own soul.

In ordinary life we hardly realize that we receive a great deal more than we give, and that it is only with gratitude that life becomes rich. It is very easy to overestimate the importance of our own achievements in comparison with what we owe others.

—*DIETRICH BONHOEFFER*

A word aptly spoken is like apples of gold in settings of silver.

Proverbs 25:11

A Moment to Refresh

An anxious heart weighs a man down, but a kind word cheers him up.

Proverbs 12:25

Give thanks in all circumstances, for this is God's will for you in Christ Jesus.

1 Thessalonians 5:18

Encourage one another and build each other up, just as in fact you are doing.

1 Thessalonians 5:11

I am a friend to all who fear you, to all who follow your precepts. The earth is filled with your love, O LORD.

Psalm 119:63–64

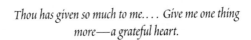

Thou has given so much to me.... Give me one thing more—a grateful heart.

—GEORGE HERBERT

The Lord is my strength and my shield; my heart trusts in him, and I am helped. My heart leaps for joy and I will give thanks to him in song.

Psalm 28:7

You turned my wailing into dancing; you removed my sackcloth and clothed me with joy, that my heart may sing to you and not be silent. O LORD my God, I will give you thanks forever.

Psalm 30:11–12

We give thanks to you, O God; we give thanks; your name is near. People tell of your wondrous deeds.

Psalm 75:1 NRSV

Gratitude is born in hearts that take time to count up past mercies.

—CHARLES EDWARD JEFFERSON

Feet in the Air

A Moment to Pause   For the busy person, a few minutes of doing nothing can be as delicious as ice cream on a hot summer day. It carries with it a sense of indulgence, of unexpected delight. And what says doin' nothin' better than sitting back and putting your feet up?

The truth is, those moments aren't indulgent at all. They provide a needed opportunity to revitalize both body and spirit. Putting your feet up is a good way to safeguard your brief time of rest and avoid the inclination to jump up and do something when the thought strikes you.

So find a comfortable place—recliner, sofa, bed, chaise longue, your desk—the choices are many. Then lean back and relax with your feet in the air. Close your eyes and let your mind drift afield. Imagine yourself running barefoot through a meadow filled with soft green grass and wild flowers. Feel the grass tickling your toes and sliding warm and soft beneath the soles of your feet. Or imagine yourself running along the beach, the sand squishing up between your toes and the cool water splashing up around your ankles. It's a vacation you can't afford to miss.

Nothing is a waste of time if you use the experience wisely.
—Rodin

A Moment to Reflect

Your mind is a wondrous creation. It can take you almost anywhere you want to go. It can offer refreshment and relaxation even in the midst of your busy day. So when you sense that your productivity is slipping, when you feel uninspired, edgy or frustrated, take your soul on a mini-vacation in your mind.

Go someplace where the air is clear and the sun is shining, someplace where you feel safe and warm and happy, someplace where you can sense the touch of God. Where is that? Lean back, put your feet in the air, and your imagination will lead you right to it.

In the midst of my harried day
when I seem farthest from myself
a moment comes to me and beckons,
"Let us fly away."

Shutting out the din
of the never-ending to-do
I close my eyes and begin
to wander in thoughts sublime,
and gather flowers in my mind.

—*Tara Afriat*

I will lie down and sleep in peace,
for you alone, O LORD,
make me dwell in safety.

Psalm 4:8

A Moment to Refresh

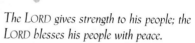

The LORD gives strength to his people; the
LORD blesses his people with peace.

Psalm 29:11

He who dwells in the shelter of the Most High
will rest in the shadow of the Almighty.

Psalm 91:1

Find rest, O my soul, in God alone; my hope
comes from him.

Psalm 62:5

Because so many people were coming and going
that they did not even have a chance to eat,
Jesus said to them, "Come with me by
yourselves to a quiet place and get some rest."

Mark 6:31

Work is not always required of a man. There is such a thing as sacred idleness, the cultivation of which is now fearfully neglected.

—GEORGE MACDONALD

The Lord said, "My presence will go with you, and I will give you rest."
Exodus 33:14 NRSV

Be at rest once more, O my soul, for the LORD has been good to you.
Psalm 116:7

The Lord said, "Six days, work is to be done, but the seventh day is a Sabbath of rest, holy to the Lord."
Exodus 31:15

This is what the Sovereign LORD, the Holy One of Israel, says: "In repentance and rest is your salvation, in quietness and trust is your strength."
Isaiah 30:15

One cannot rest except after steady practice.

—GEORGE ADE

Stretch! Stretch! Stretch!

A Moment to Pause   The human body is amazing. Though it consists of little more than mass, muscle, and matter, God has created it to act and react in unison with the soul. Dancers, for example, have long understood the tenacious link between body and soul—the glory of moving one while moving the other.

You can feel the effects of moving body and soul without becoming a ballerina. It only takes a little stretching and bending. Find a place where you feel comfortable. It doesn't matter if that place is in the backyard, at the gym, in the middle of the living room, or in the privacy of the bedroom. Slowly focus on one limb, one muscle at a time, stretching carefully just until you sense that your body is waking up and releasing its stiffness.

Bend from the waist and then from the side. Lift your arms above your head and stretch them as high as you can. Lock your fingers together and push up onto your tiptoes. As you move, your body will begin to release pent-up tension and stress. Relax and move, relax and move, until your body and soul are singing together. When you're finished, take a few minutes to rest and enjoy your inner harmony.

Better to bend than break.
—Scottish Proverb

A Moment to Reflect

*I*f you find it difficult to loosen up and stretch in your worldview, in your personal vision and creativity, in your interaction with others, stretch–stretch–stretching your arms and legs and learning to twist and turn and bend may be just the right place to start.

As you reach with your arms, reach with your heart and soul as well, asking God to help you find new perspectives, new approaches, and new solutions to old problems. You might be surprised to learn how many opportunities come your way when you begin to stretch and bend with the challenges in your life.

Whenever I go running
Across the rugged ground,
My legs stretch out before me
And my heart begins to pound.

My arms pump quickly up and down
In rhythm at my side
And my spirit lifts within me
Overjoyed with the ride.

My lungs burn ever so slightly
Breathing in the morning air
And my soul vibrates with happiness
Releasing every care.

—*Tara Afriat*

God did this so that men would seek him and perhaps reach out for him and find him, though he is not far from each one of us. "For in him we live and move and have our being."

Acts 17:27–28

A Moment to Refresh

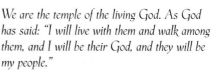

We are the temple of the living God. As God has said: "I will live with them and walk among them, and I will be their God, and they will be my people."

2 Corinthians 6:16

Whether you turn to the right or to the left, your ears will hear a voice behind you, saying, "This is the way; walk in it."

Isaiah 30:21

The Lord says, "Forget the former things; do not dwell on the past. See, I am doing a new thing! Now it springs up; do you not perceive it? I am making a way in the desert and streams in the wasteland."

Isaiah 43:18–19

The human body is a machine which winds its own springs: the living image of perpetual motion.

—JULIEN OFFROY DE LA METTRIE

The LORD Almighty has purposed and who can thwart him? His hand is stretched out, and who can turn it back?

Isaiah 14:27

The LORD gives strength to the weary and increases the power of the weak.

Isaiah 40:29

Prepare your minds for action; be self-controlled; set your hope fully on the grace to be given you when Jesus Christ is revealed.

1 Peter 1:13

There is a time for everything, and a season for every activity under heaven.

Ecclesiastes 3:1

Life is not merely being alive, but being well.

—MARTIAL

Breathe In! Breathe Out!

A Moment to Pause Inhale. Exhale. Inhale. Exhale. It's the rhythm of life, and yet it passes without effort, without thinking. Each breath is a miracle, blessing our bodies and brains with the oxygen that brings life and sustenance. Perhaps that's why focused, deep breathing has such a calming, strengthening effect on both the body and the soul.

The beauty of this exercise is that you don't need a special place or time to draw on its rich benefits. Just about anyplace is appropriate—in the middle of your busy day, as you wait to pick up your children, as you sit in a busy board meeting, even as you make a presentation. Simply take a deep breath, hold it for five seconds, and breathe out slowly through your nose. Do this once or several times in a row. As your lungs fill, oxygen rushes into your bloodstream and is carried to your brain and extremities. No one even needs to know that you are taking an oxygen break.

The results are instantaneous. You will quickly feel your nerves relaxing, your mood lifting, your fatigue abating—just by consciously doing what comes naturally.

The Lord God formed the man from the dust of the ground and breathed into his nostrils the breath of life, and the man became a living being.

—Genesis 2:7

A Moment to Reflect

Each breath you take is a gift of life from God himself—an expression of his love for you and a reminder of his moment-by-moment commitment to you. How marvelous that he would invest so much in a simple, natural act.

If you have ever wondered if God cares about you, whether he is interested in the smallest details of your life, now you know. If you have ever wondered if he really wants to be part of your life every moment of every day, the answer is as close as your next breath. God loves you. Breathe deeply and ponder that wonderful fact.

One breath for every moment
The proof of life's bright flame,
Flowing always in and out,
Every day the same.

One breath for every moment
Sustaining life so sweet.
Giving strength to words and thoughts
While keeping up the beat.

One breath for every moment
A gift of God so true
Making each a living soul
As only God can do.

—TARA AFRIAT

By the word of the LORD were the heavens made, their starry host by the breath of his mouth.

Psalm 33:6

A Moment to Refresh

Let everything that has breath praise the LORD. Praise the LORD.

Psalm 150:6

I praise you because I am fearfully and wonderfully made; your works are wonderful, I know that full well.

Psalm 139:14

This is what God the Lord says—he who created the heavens and stretched them out, who spread out the earth and all that comes out of it, who gives breath to its people, and life to those who walk on it: "I, the Lord, have called you in righteousness; I will take hold of your hand. I will keep you and will make you to be a covenant for the people and a light for the Gentiles."

Isaiah 42:5–6

The hand of God is strong enough to protect His feeblest child,

yet gentle enough to lead that same child homeward.

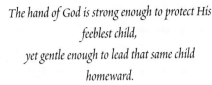

Melinda Mahand

How precious to me are your thoughts, O God! How vast is the sum of them! Were I to count them, they would outnumber the grains of sand.

Psalm 139:17–18

Jesus said, "Peace be with you! As the Father has sent me, I am sending you." And with that he breathed on them and said, "Receive the Holy Spirit."

John 20:21–22

Jesus said, "I came that they may have life, and have it to the full."

John 10:10

All scripture is God–breathed and is useful for teaching, rebuking, correcting and training in righteousness, so that the man of God may be thoroughly equipped for every good work.

2 Timothy 3:16–17

The life force is vigorous. The delight that accompanies it counter-balances all the pains and hardships that confront men. It makes life worth living.

—W. Somerset Maugham

Name Them One by One

A Moment to Pause

God is good—very good! Even in the bad times, he showers you with reminders that he loves you with an everlasting love. When you take time to consider those reminders and see them for what they really are, your soul is nourished and you realize that you are rich indeed!

Wherever you happen to be right now, take a few minutes to consider your life and the blessings God has poured out on you. Take an inventory, speaking each one aloud and thanking him for it. Close your eyes and visualize each person God has placed in your life and speak each name aloud. Include even those who challenge you and keep you from getting too comfortable, for they were sent to bless you as well. When you have finished, move on to those things that provide you with hope—things like forgiveness and eternal life. Even hope itself is a blessing, for without it we would not have the courage or the will to become all that God intends.

So get started counting up those blessings. If you run out of time, just wait for the next opportunity to take a break and start again where you left off.

If you count all your assets, you always show a profit.
——Robert Quillen

A Moment to Reflect

No matter what is taking place in your life right now, there are always blessings to count—more than you might imagine. And at those times when you feel you have the least to celebrate, your soul receives the greatest benefit.

Whatever your situation might be, whether there are blue skies or gray holding court over your life, do your soul a favor—start counting. Soon you will feel a soothing shower of God's love filling your soul's empty chambers to overflowing, and you will realize how much you really have and how very much God has given you.

This morning light
Splashing across the hills and
illuminating the sky,
So singularly beautiful, it seems a gift
meant just for me.
God's simple blessing.

This newborn day
Offering up an unblemished canvas,
an unwritten book
So singularly unique, it seems it was
made just for me.
God's simple blessing.

—TARA AFRIAT

The LORD is good and his love endures forever; his faithfulness continues through all generations.

Psalm 100:5

A Moment to Refresh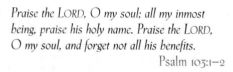

Praise the LORD, O my soul; all my inmost being, praise his holy name. Praise the LORD, O my soul, and forget not all his benefits.

Psalm 103:1–2

I will praise you forever for what you have done; in your name I will hope, for your name is good. I will praise you in the presence of your saints.

Psalm 52:9

I will sacrifice a freewill offering to you; I will praise your name, O LORD, for it is good. For he has delivered me from all my troubles, and my eyes have looked in triumph on my foes.

Psalm 54:6–7

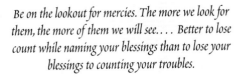

Be on the lookout for mercies. The more we look for them, the more of them we will see.... Better to lose count while naming your blessings than to lose your blessings to counting your troubles.

—MALTBIE D. BABCOCK

Praise the LORD, for the LORD is good;
sing praise to his name, for that is pleasant.
Psalm 135:3

We know that in all things God works for
the good of those who love him, who have
been called according to his purpose.
Romans 8:28

Blessings crown the head of the righteous.
Proverbs 10:6

The LORD bless you and keep you; the
Lord make his face shine upon you and be
gracious to you; the LORD turn his face
toward you and give you peace.
Numbers 6:24–26

Taste and see that the LORD is good; blessed is the man who takes refuge in him.

—PSALM 34:8

All the Colors of the Rainbow

As if the blue of the sky and the rich colors of the landscape were not enough, God forged the rainbow. It is perhaps the most incredible artistic masterpiece ever rendered. God has given you all the colors of the rainbow as well—color to transform the world, color to inspire one's senses, color to stir and refresh one's soul.

Even if your people look like stickmen and your horses look like... well, not like horses, you can still find moments of soulful retreat by creating your own colorful artwork. Find yourself a sheet of paper and crayons, colored pencils, watercolors, markers, anything that will give you the freedom you need. Then lose yourself for a few minutes in the exuberant world of blues and greens, reds and yellows, and pinks and purples. Forget about the traditional color combinations and experiment with your own. Your picture can be a rendering of something that has snagged your interest or a free-form collection of colorful splashes and streaks.

As you work, put your heart into it, letting your eyes absorb the brilliance of the shades and tones until you can feel your soul flying. Then sit back and take a look at what you have created.

Every artist dips his brush in his own soul,
and paints his own nature into his pictures.
—Henry Ward Beecher

A Moment to Reflect

Sometimes your soul needs rest, and sometimes it needs stimulation to keep it fresh and healthy. Engaging in colorful, artistic exercises is like opening the drapes and letting the sun shine bright and pure through a spotless windowpane. All you need is right in your hand.

Art nourishes the soul—in its creation as much as in its appreciation. If your soul could use a splash of color, pick up a brush, a crayon or a pencil. Your adventure in art may not belong on the wall of an art museum, but chances are it will look right at home on the refrigerator.

The world's great canvas is offered up
through the myriad expressions of our eyes.
Speak and our words weave worlds
divine as a brushstroke reveals mountains and skies
of which we have never dreamed.
Sing and the strains fill our souls
with the magic of light and color
and shapes and movement
as yet unimagined by our minds.
Bow and our praise adorns the tabernacle of God,
lifting our souls to heavenly heights from which
we will descend only when we must.

—TARA AFRIAT

113

God said to Noah, "I have set my rainbow in the clouds, and it will be the sign of the covenant between me and the earth."

Genesis 9:13

A Moment to Refresh

The word of the LORD came to Ezekiel the priest.... Like the appearance of a rainbow in the clouds on a rainy day, so was the radiance around him. This was the appearance of the likeness of the glory of the LORD.

Ezekiel 1:3, 28

God said to Noah, "Whenever I bring clouds over the earth and the rainbow appears in the clouds, I will remember my covenant between me and you and all living creatures of every kind. Never again will the waters become a flood to destroy all life."

Genesis 9:14–15

Lift your eyes and look to the heavens: Who created all these? He who brings out the starry host one by one, and calls them each by name. Because of his great power and mighty strength, not one of them is missing.

Isaiah 40:26

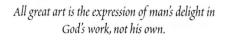

All great art is the expression of man's delight in God's work, not his own.

❧

—JOHN RUSKIN

You created my inmost being; you knit me together in my mother's womb.

Psalm 139:13

Ezekiel said, I saw visions of God.... I looked, and, behold, a whirlwind came out of the north, a great cloud, and a fire infolding itself, and a brightness was about it, and out of the midst thereof as the colour of amber, out of the midst of the fire.

Ezekiel 1:1, 4 KJV

The Mighty One, God, the Lord, speaks and summons the earth from the rising of the sun to the place where it sets. From Zion, perfect in beauty, God shines forth.

Psalm 50:1–2

A man should hear a little music, read a little poetry, and see a fine picture every day of his life, in order that worldly cares may not obliterate the sense of the beautiful which God has implanted in the human soul.

❧

—JOHANN WOLFGANG VON GOETHE

Write It Down

A Moment to Pause

When you write things down, it is usually so that you won't forget them—words on paper to organize fleeting thoughts. But there are other important reasons to write things down. One is that doing so creates an enduring retreat for the soul.

Keeping a journal has long been a cherished activity. Many people, young and old, rich and poor, famous and obscure have understood the power of writing their thoughts as a way of caring for their souls. Your journal can be as simple as a spiral notebook or as fancy as a cloth-covered tome. And you can take as much time or as little as your schedule allows. As you write, forget about style and grammar, spelling and punctuation. Just write as your heart speaks to you, delving down deep into your soul.

Writing can help you discover so many wonderful things about yourself. It can help you identify your gifts and talents, those things that bring joy and fulfillment to your life. It can help you gain perspective and discover aspects of your temperament and personality that you never knew existed. Let your pen lead the way.

In a very real sense, the writer writes in order to
teach himself.
—Alfred Kazin

A Moment to Reflect

Writing your thoughts is a valuable tool for unburdening your soul, sorting out solutions, and creating a record of personal and spiritual growth. And writing your thoughts makes you feel good.

If you have never stopped to feel the warmth of a pen in your hand, to feel it slide smoothly across the paper, it could be time for you to discover this pleasant and therapeutic art. Select an appealing paper, a soothing color of ink, a naturally lighted corner, and a cozy chair. Now pick up a pen and refresh your soul.

Let me trace my hope in symbols,
Let me move mountains within a phrase.
Emotion's turbulent core,
so threateningly close within,
now becomes benign
under the taming of my pen.

Let me compose the letters of my heart
Let me ascribe them to beauty and delight,
The lament of sorrow,
so threateningly close within,
now becomes benign
under the taming of my pen.

—TARA AFRIAT

The LORD said to Moses, "Write down these words, for in accordance with these words I have made a covenant with you and with Israel."

Exodus 34:27

A Moment to Refresh

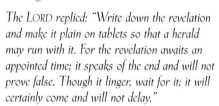

The LORD replied: "Write down the revelation and make it plain on tablets so that a herald may run with it. For the revelation awaits an appointed time; it speaks of the end and will not prove false. Though it linger, wait for it; it will certainly come and will not delay."

Habakkuk 2:2–3

The apostle Luke wrote: Since I myself have carefully investigated everything from the beginning, it seemed good also to me to write an orderly account for you.... so that you may know the certainty of the things you have been taught.

Luke 1:3–4

I, Paul, write this greeting in my own hand.

1 Corinthians 16:21

A poem, a sentence, causes us to see ourselves. I be, and I see my being, at the same time.

—Ralph Waldo Emerson

My brothers, rejoice in the Lord! It is no trouble for me to write the same things to you again, and it is a safeguard for you.
Philippians 3:1

The apostle John wrote: I write these things to you who believe in the name of the Son of God so that you may know that you have eternal life.
1 John 5:13

The apostle John wrote: I do not write to you because you do not know the truth, but because you do know it and because no lie comes from the truth.
1 John 2:21

He who was seated on the throne said, "I am making everything new!" Then he said, "Write this down, for these words are trustworthy and true."
Revelation 21:5

There is no lighter burden, nor more agreeable, than a pen.

—Petrarch

Dare to Dream

The dreams you dream in your mind's eye are a prelude to greatness. They challenge, inspire, and give purpose to your life. Taking time out to dream of what could be is an invigorating exercise.

In the midst of your long, busy day, set aside a few minutes to rise above your daily involvements and regimens and let your soul fly free. If you can, find a comfortable place to do your dreaming. Take a walk in the park during your lunch break, settle in with a cup of tea while your children are napping, or just turn off the television and soak in the silence for a few minutes.

Once you're comfortable, turn your thoughts to what you enjoy most. If it's golf, imagine yourself as a great golfer; if it's business, imagine your enterprise thriving beyond your greatest expectations. If it's being a great mom or dad, see yourself developing new ways to draw out the potential in each of your children. As your dreams take shape, don't just dash off to the next thing, stay for a while. The first step to making your dreams come true is to make them your own.

Cherish your visions and your dreams as they are the children of your soul; the blueprints of your ultimate achievements.
—*Napoleon Hill*

A Moment to Reflect

Dreaming keeps hope alive in your life. And hope is to the soul what water is to the body. It refreshes and renews.

If you need to see the sunshine at the end of a long, cloudy day, if you have felt the joy of living slipping through your fingers, a dream fest might be just the retreat for you. Get started right away, and give yourself time, because most dreams develop over time. And remember to ask God to inspire your dreams. He is eager to fill your heart with the full intent of his marvelous plans for your life.

As I was sitting all alone
A star in yonder window shone
And led me to a place quite lovely
Where all my dreams circled above me

Each one was close enough to touch
Each goal that I desired so much
And hope soared high within my soul
I can't say why. I just know that I know.

Doubts and fears assail me still
But I stay near that window sill
And focus on that brilliant star
For that is where my victories are.

—Roberta S. Cully

We are God's workmanship, created in Christ Jesus to do good works, which God prepared in advance for us to do.

Ephesians 2:10

A Moment to Refresh

It is God who works in you to will and to act according to his good purpose.

Philippians 2:13

This is what was spoken by the prophet Joel: "In the last days, God says, I will pour out my Spirit on all people. Your sons and daughters will prophesy, your young men will see visions, your old men will dream dreams."

Acts 2:16–17

The word of the LORD came to Abram in a vision: "Do not be afraid, Abram. I am your shield, your very great reward."

Genesis 15:1

Dream the impossible dream. Dreaming it may make it possible. It often has.

※

—AUTHOR UNKNOWN

The path of the righteous is like the first gleam of dawn, shining ever brighter till the full light of day.

Proverbs 4:18

During the night the mystery was revealed to Daniel in a vision.

Daniel 2:19

May the God of hope fill you with all joy and peace as you trust in him, so that you may overflow with hope by the power of the Holy Spirit.

Romans 15:13

Wisdom is sweet to your soul; if you find it, there is a future hope for you, and your hope will not be cut off.

Proverbs 24:14

Vision encompasses vast vistas outside the realm of the predictable, the safe, the expected.

※

—CHARLES SWINDOLL

God Thoughts

A Moment to Pause Nothing has the power to lift the soul from this earthly realm to heavenly heights like filling your mind with thoughts of your great Creator. Part worship and part prayer, thoughts of God are reminders that you are loved and watched over. They allay fears and anxieties. They celebrate life over death, victory over defeat, joy over sorrow.

Settle back and close your eyes. Let your mind reflect on God's greatness, his power, and his majesty. Then consider a few of God's characteristics—love, joy, peace, patience, kindness, goodness, faithfulness, gentleness, self-control. Reflect how God's love has touched your life, how his peace has touched your life, his joy, his patience, his kindness, and so forth. As these thoughts evoke emotions, don't hesitate to express them. Free the tears of thanksgiving, the smiles of joy, the sighs of peace and let them wash over your soul.

As you focus on God thoughts, feel yourself soaring above the cares of the day, looking at things with a new perspective, gaining strength, and experiencing a resurgence of creativity.

The thought of God is never a burden;
it is a gentle breeze which bears us up, a hand which
supports us and raises us,
a light which guides us, and a spirit which vivifies us
though we do not feel its working.
—Francesco Malaval

God's thoughts are always about you. When your thoughts are on him, a connection is made—a connection that heals and refreshes and rejoices the soul. If your thoughts keep you earthbound, focus them on the one who transcends the affairs of this world. If your thoughts leave you feeling mortal and unworthy, turn them to the one who has given you eternal life and made you worthy to be called his child.

God is pleased when you think about him because he knows that doing so will fill your soul with hope and change your life.

Was it hope deferred
or a dream once loved, now lost
that led me to this valley
of dark, despairing thoughts?

It is only the thought of You,
of Your gentle Spirit and unfailing love,
that guides my spirit home again
upon the wings of a Dove.

—TARA AFRIAT

Cast all your anxiety on him because he cares for you.

1 Peter 5:7

A Moment to Refresh

Great is the Lord, and most worthy of praise, in the city of our God, his holy mountain. It is beautiful in its loftiness, the joy of the whole earth.

Psalm 48:1–2

On my bed I remember you; I think of you through the watches of the night. Because you are my help, I sing in the shadow of your wings.

Psalm 63:6–7

To be spiritually minded is life and peace.

Romans 8:6 KJV

My Christian friends, who also have been called by God! Think of Jesus, whom God sent to be the High Priest we profess.

Hebrews 3:1 GNT

I want to know God's thoughts; the rest are details.

—ALBERT EINSTEIN

*Great is the Lord and most worthy of
praise; his greatness no one can fathom.*
                                        Psalm 145:3

*When anxiety was great within me, your
consolation brought joy to my soul.*
                                        Psalm 94:19

*Whatever is true, whatever is noble,
whatever is right, whatever is pure,
whatever is lovely, whatever is admirable—
if anything is excellent or praiseworthy—
think about such things.*
                                        Philippians 4:8

*Let us have confidence, then, and approach
God's throne where there is grace. There
we will receive mercy and find grace to help
us just when we need it.*
                                        Hebrews 4:16 GNT

*Certain thoughts
are prayers. There
are moments when
whatever the
attitude of the body,
the soul is on its
knees.*

—VICTOR HUGO

Other books in the Soul Retreats™ series:

Soul Retreats™ for Moms
Soul Retreats™ for Teachers
Soul Retreats™ for Women

All available from your favorite bookstore.
We would like to hear from you.
Please send your comments about this book to:

Inspirio™, *the gift group of Zondervan*
Attn: Product Development
Grand Rapids, Michigan 49530
www.inspirio.com

<u>*Our mission:*</u>
To produce distinctively Christian gifts that point people to God's Word
with refreshing messages and innovative designs.

inspirio™